miracles infinite...

Foreword by Megha Bajaj, Chitra Prasad & Arjun Rajagopalan

Akshara Hariharan

Made with ♥ on the Notion Press Platform
www.notionpress.com

I dedicate this book to my parents for giving me wings to fly, and to my Mahatria for being my source of faith and making me believe in things I could not see yet!

Contents

Notes from the Author

It gives me immense pleasure to present this piece of work. I would like to express my heartfelt gratitude to my family, friends, and my mentor for being my source of strength throughout this process.

Why miracles infinite?
I began finding solace in words when I was as young as 13. I have always felt that I can express myself better through writing. When the idea of creating my poetry book sprouted, I aimed to keep it simple, relatable, and real.

When we contemplate what makes life beautiful, it's not something colossal that happens once in a while. The joy of life resides in the little things around us. All we need for a wholesome life is a splash of self-love, a handful of beautiful relationships, rays of divine touch, and epiphanies we pick along the way. If we weave these elements together and look at life, it's nothing short of an infinite set of miracles. Hence, miracles infinite is a collection of short poems that you can read one at a time and resonate with.

Happy reading.
Loving you all so much,
Akshara Hariharan.

Foreword

The very name Akshara, has Akshar in it. Akshar means letters. So, it's not much of a surprise that Akshara is releasing her first anthology of poetry at this young age. Words flow from her, and through her and she is someone who finds meaning to herself and her life, through her words.

When Akshara first joined the WoW Online Writing and Healing workshop with me, I saw a girl wants to unleash her thoughts and feelings through words. However, over time, I saw her grow. As a person. A professional. A seeker. And an author. Suddenly her words contained so much more depth. They seemed more measured. More authentic. And yes, more impactful.

Miracles infinite is a collection of life poetry. It is a condensation of one person's experiences and yet, as you read it, you will find so much of your thoughts and feelings in them. Self-love, something so close to so many of us is dwelled deeply upon, as Akshara grows in self-love herself. God, is a recurring theme as Akshara discovers, and often rediscovers, her own relationship with God. I think as Akshara observed people, and her relationships with them, so many poetries were born.

This book is real because it is her experience of finding herself. Her voice. Her calm, within the chaos. As someone who has both her left and right brain very much in place (A Chartered accountant who also writes poetry), I find her words refreshing and her insights presenting food for thought.

I see Akshara soaring to great heights as a person, and a professional and especially as an author. Her maiden book is filled with honesty and innocence, exploration and discovery and I believe you will find a little part of her in you, and you in her.

Read the poems, ponder over them. Allow them to become a part of you.
Wishing Akshara greater heights, and depths…

Megha Bajaj
National Bestselling Author,
Author-Mentor, Edupreneur and above all, a seeker.
www.MeghaBajajWoW.com

Akshara, the creative poet and hardworking, intelligent student turned professional, has brought out journeys of all those motivated youngsters who dream big. It always starts with a dream; however, what differentiates a successful person is his or her ability to stay persistent, positive, self-assured, and, most importantly, deal with relationships and self with empathy and honesty.

The simple poems have such deep messages, and if one follows them, he or she will always be a happy soul and spread happiness around. My favorite phrases from the book would stay etched with me, and I will always teach my kids and youngsters around me. This book reiterates the need to learn, unlearn, and be flexible.

The poems hold so true in every aspect of our lives, right from childhood to adulthood, personal to professional lives.

Arjun Rajagoplan
Partner, Deloitte India.

When you withdraw your senses, you can experience your Creator; and when you look around, you can connect with His creations. Poetry is born from within and manifests as words in the world outside. It is an experience set to rhyme and rhythm. It is the inner flowering of the soul, holding a mirror to your thoughts and feelings.

One such deep and divine experience is the collection of poems written by Akshara Hariharan, titled Miracles Infinite. Life goes through a kaleidoscope of experiences. It begins with self-love, which helps us establish relationships. The self-awareness in us makes us notice the epiphanies life gifts us. The wise will turn it into an opportunity, making it an ever since moment in life.

Punctuate your busy day with moments to pause and ponder, to reflect and to dwell. There is beautiful poetry in each of us that the world is waiting to hear. The poet in Akshara is one such dimension of her personality—a Chartered Accountant who counts numbers and a poet who makes her life count. I am absolutely overwhelmed to see the little child that I have known emerge from within as a poet par excellence.

Chitra Prasad
Correspondent, NSN Group of Schools.

Self-Love

Growth is all about
catching up with the most broken part of you
and whispering to yourself,
'How it happened doesn't matter anymore,
because you need to shed some pieces
in order to sculpt your finest version.'

-growth

I just want to work hard enough
without giving up
so that all the women that I have once been
find victory in witnessing everything that they ever
dreamt of
in every bit of what I am today!

-dreams

The version of me that I most cherish
is not the one that has it all together,
but the one that's shattered into pieces
yet trying to piece itself together, once again
resilient enough to rise till the end of time!

–cherishing me

Behind every successful person,
there's a little one that dared to dream big and
raise the bars.
That version of us deserves to be celebrated
because there's no way any of us could have made it
alone!

-thankful!

Don't restrict yourself too much.
By the time you set yourself free,
You might have forgotten how to fly.
The sky is yours too.
Spread your wings and explore while you still can!

–embracing me

Self-love starts with
befriending that part of yours
you wish never existed.

-befriending self

Even after knowing all of what followed,
if I had to get lost
in order to reunite with my true self,
I would do it a million times,
only difference this time
I would do it unapologetically.

–live your way

Learn to love yourself
when you still smell of
self-doubts and fears
because the darkest nights will often be spent alone.

–self-help

Enough of running ahead of yourself.
Perhaps it's time to feel …
the tears beneath the heavy eyelids you've been brushing aside,
the emotions behind the long silence you've been observing,
the fears hidden behind the unreconciled thoughts you've been fighting.
Gear down for a while,
catch your breath,
feel the pause.
Life is what happens between two heartbeats.
Enough of running ahead of yourself.
Perhaps it's time to feel.

–catch up

I realised
if it led me to where I am today,
anything that I have ever been
could have never been a mistake.
It's how life happened
and it finally synced.

-guiltfree

On any given day,
never apologise
for being yourself.

–be yourself

What if for a change
I woke up to every dawn
shredding my fears a little more,
ripping off the self-doubts gobbling me from within,
and nipping the language of 'I can't' altogether?

What if for a change
I glided through the days
believing in myself a little more,
embracing myself as I am,
and brimming with a gush of positivity all day?

What if for a change
I recollected often,
am not ahead, not behind, and not in a race?
Taking it slow and letting it go a little
are absolutely okay.

What if for a change
I had it engraved in me
it's okay if I wasn't successful
or pleasing all the time,
but it's not okay if I wasn't me all the while?

-unlearning

Do you know me at all?
I am not
the tone of my skin,
the texture of my hair,
the robes I drape,
or the past I left behind.

I am
the thoughts I conceive,
the smiles I spread,
the dreams I envision,
and the pain I heal myself from.

My flaws and insecurities
define me not,
although the lens through which I tackle them
surely do!

I am not
what you see,
what you hear,
or what you know of me.
I am much more than just all of that and beyond.
Do you know me at all?

–it's me

I take some time out, once in a way ,
and let everything around me snooze for a while
so that I get to know a part of me
that still remains a stranger to me.

I take some time out, once in a way,
unhide the wounds that I am trying to veil,
go through the emotions I have been bottling up for
ages,
and accept that part of me I have been running away
from.

I take some time out, once in a way,
unpack how I feel,
and embrace every tiny piece of me,
for it draws me closer to myself.

-unstrange

I chose to do away with the problems that exist only in my head,
I chose to do away with people that do not know if I exist,
I chose to do away with my past that's gone far.
Thence, I am happy.

I chose to embrace the things that find their way into my life,
I chose to gracefully let go of things that find their way out,
I chose to smile as I walk down the streets that I don't belong in.
Thence, I am happy.

I chose to give more, expect less, and judge none,
I chose to perceive less, accept more, and complain nil,
I chose to celebrate together, heal alone, and enjoy myself.
Thence, I am happy.

I am happy with where I am
and how I made it through.
Thence, happiness found me!

–happiness found me!

I know a day being designed, not too far off,
where I no longer need any reassurance from others
because I am self-assured by accepting the parts in me
that are not the best by far.

I know a day being designed, not too far off,
where I no longer lie to myself that I feel all okay
because I am willing to feel my emotions.

I know a day being designed, not too far off,
where I no longer feel insecure about flaws
because I know I am still complete even with little
mistakes.

I know a day being designed, not too far off,
where I no longer have to remind myself of the battles I
fought
because I see resilience in the prettiest smile being
flashed in my reflection after all.

–designing destiny

There's a part of me that is
hurting,
dwindling,
and
still healing.
That's also the part of me
that you will never get to see
because
I celebrate together
and heal alone.

-healing

Relationships

You will never know what you mean to me.
Your arms are where I broke down the most,
your laps are where I have had my deepest slumbers,
your shoulders carried me the farthest thus far,
your eyes shed the most tears for me, and
your hands were always one of the first to lift me
whenever I fell.
For all I know,
time can only separate you and me
but not you from me
because you taught me almost everything
but to love you enough.

-parental love

Falling in love with the way
someone thinks
is a whole other level of attraction.
Anything else
will wear off with time.

–thinking right

If there is ever a thing that you'd like to gift me,
let it be quality time
because
it's something only you could gift me
or I won't have it at all.

–love language

We were too busy
loving each other as we were
that with time
we lost track of
the differences we share,
the flaws we have,
and the immaterial things in between too.

-ignoring flaws

I want to be around during your rough days
so that when you are mourning over the lesser side
I will be there to remind you of the better side
that's still a part of you.

-grateful

I wish to linger around till the finishing line,
refresh your memory when it starts to fade,
and help you relive your good old memories
just by shuttling you across ages.

-reliving memories

I know
you are not the same person that
you once were,
but neither am I
because in togetherness we evolve and
we never agreed to accept just one shade of each other
in the first place.

–change

Amid our differences,
we are meant to explore life together
because a part of you belongs to me and a part of me belongs to you.
How else will we complete each other without celebrating our differences?
Perhaps, it's life way of gifting us a new world.

–celebrating differences

Will you be the one
who believes in me when no one else does?
Will you be the one
who trusts me without seeking any explanation?
Will you be the one
who accepts me with the flaws I possess?
Will you be the one
who sees me beyond what I was in the past?
Will you be the one
who hears me out without judging me?
Will you be the one
who makes me feel not alone through the peaks and valleys?
Will you be the one
who makes me feel special in the entire world?
Will you be the one
who can hold me together when I am falling apart?
Will you be the one
with whom I can be myself?

-will you?

Would you tell me?
I want to hear from you …
the memories you hold close to your heart
and also the untold secret that's hurting you within.
Tell me … it heals.

Would you let me accompany you?
I want to travel with you …
all the way to fulfil your dreams,
and also through the days that challenge you.
Let me accompany you … it makes the journey
interesting.

Would you be yourself with me?
I want to accept you as you are …
with the lovely traits you have imbibed
and also the flaws that complete you.
Be yourself … trust me it brings me closer to you.

-until forever

I am here to express myself to you,
share my dreams with you
and insecurities too
’cause it’s a new dawn, giving us a rebirth.

I am here to be my vulnerable self with you,
express my unravelled emotions,
and feel closer to us
’cause it’s a new dawn, showering us another chance.

I am here to make ‘us’ my priority,
Gift you the time of my day,
listen to all your words and silence too
’cause it’s a new dawn, gifting some togetherness again.

I am here to forget the past,
Embrace changes,
and refurbish our life
’cause it’s a new dawn, bestowing one more day to our life.

–building ‘Us’

Have I told you yet?
Whenever I am grim,
all I want to do is hit your line.
Your reassuring tone
makes me feel I can combat anything.

Have I told you yet?
Every time I conquer,
all I want to do is look for you.
Your quarter smile
makes me feel all that I battled is worth it.

Have I told you yet?
Whenever I feel out of place,
all I want to do is be in your arms.
Your warmth
makes me feel everything will soon fall into place.

Have I told you yet?
Whenever I am alone,
all I want to do is think of you.
My silence
makes me experience you within me …

–feeling loved

Let there be talks and exchange of thoughts,
yet let there be silence too
for it shall add rhythm to the communication.

Let there be proximity and intimacy,
yet let there be some personal space too
for it shall reflect the beauty of oneness.

Let there be fun and grin,
yet let there be tears too
for it shall make the bond stronger.

Let there be care and shield,
yet let there be trust too
for it shall give wings to a secure relationship.

let there be joy in togetherness,
not suffocation,
in the name of love.

–togetherness

Let's celebrate the days that were a total ten.
Let's also celebrate the days that we barely glided through
and the days in-between; let's celebrate the joy of
nothing.
Pause for a while; let's unbox life, one day at a time.

Let's create a million happy moments together
sometimes just by talking the entire night away
about the old memories, the unaccomplished desires,
and also about the pain that's niggling within.
Pause for a while; let's unbox life, one moment at a time.

Let's spice up the journey with some unplanned trips.
Perhaps, let's get lost in the cold streets on a winter night
with small talks and twinkling smiles, until the dawn
cracks.
Pause for a while; let's unbox life, one experience at a
time.

Let's unfear.
We are stronger than you know.
Pause for a while; let's unbox life, together!

–unboxing life

When I say I love you,
all I mean is
your happiness is my happiness,
what makes you sad disturbs me too,
your insecurities are no more just yours,
and your dreams shall be mine too.
With love we shall weather all storms whatsoever,
but let there not be one suggesting we both have been
loving the same person all the while.

-love

No pain is permanent.
Everything is bound to fade with time.
A few just takes longer than the rest,
but for the days in between
I will be around, take your hands into mine,
and get you through this
expecting nothing but see you smile!

-selfless

Even after everything else slips away,
we are still left with memories,
so never regret for something
that made you love once.

-memories

Divinity

I still could not fathom out how
I trusted the path I did not know and
reached out to things that I could not see,
but now that I have come through it all
I know I was not alone all the while!

–never alone

I see you, God,
in every happy face with a brimming smile,
in every innocent laughter,
and in every celebration of joy of little things in life.

I hear you, God,
in every voice of love,
in every word of truth,
and in every whisper of prayer.

I feel you, God,
in every touch of love,
in every embrace of care,
and in every act of kindness.

I experience you, God.
in every pure thought I conceive,
in every breath of silence,
and in every step I take towards the unknown with surrender.

–He's here!

I beg to differ
that He cannot be seen
because
it's Him that I see in
every piece of universe
and
every slice of sky.

-ubiquitous

I know I have healed enough
when I no longer feel like reminding myself
I am doing just fine!

-divine rays

If you can notice someone in pain and realize something within you suffers,
beauty is compassion.
If you can listen to what others have to say without being opinionated,
beauty is patience.
If you can stay silent when you have nothing sensible to utter in an argument,
beauty is silence.
If you can deal with a catastrophe without taking it to heart,
beauty is acceptance.
If you can love someone enough to let them go in pursuit of their dreams,
beauty is love
If you can let go of your personal interest for the sake of greater good,
beauty is sacrifice.
If you can admire others' beauty and feel beautiful about yourself,
beauty is just a reflection of you.

-beauty

Day by day
I choose to be more divine than human
because I don't want to know
what my days are like without Him.

-grace

When you can embrace
things that cannot be changed,
the feel within
is the closest to heaven
you can buy on earth.

–heaven on earth

I asked Him,
'If you have already given me all that I am ever going to need,
then why will I ever turn to you?'

He replied,
'Because there will be days
when you will forget
who you are and what you are made of!'

-surrender

I cherish those days
when everything about me was left to Him
because those were the days
I felt most secure,
doubted myself less,
trusted the way ahead,
and more importantly,
reflected my best self!

–everything of Him

When I am made of hundreds of thousands of things
that could easily slip away in a fraction of a second
yet everything remains intact,
for all I've known
there couldn't be a reason more satisfying than Him.

–His grace

Even if it's just one moment in this lifetime
that I will get to dissolve into Him,
I will live my entire life
making myself worthy of it!

–dissolve into Him

When I look back,
everything I have ever loved once
at some level
reflected some shade of Him.

-creation

How long have I been searching for You outside,
when You already reside within me?

How often have I enunciated new verses and chants,
oblivious that a little bit of silence could lead me to You?

How many times have I ransacked the whole of earth in
pursuit of the best offering,
when all You need is some devotion?

How much have I wept for a loss,
not knowing You have something better in store for me?

How hard have I been holding on to the wrong
opportunities in despair,
ignorant that You will never let me fall?

How anxious have I been spending my days, worrying
about the future,
incognizant that I will never be left alone when You are
around?

Still, I know it's You walking along, holding me tight
because with every step I take towards You,
I feel closer to myself!

–voyage within

He brewed each of us with unique ingredients
and never expected any of us to taste like one another
just so that we could season earth with our own flavours
to make it wholesome and delightful.
Then why on earth do we try hard to mirror each other?

–uniqueness

With every ounce of joy you experience,
He brims with celebration.
With every pinch of pain you endure,
He sheds silent tears, healing you.
With every grain of piece, you get shattered into,
He puts you back together, even stronger.
With every swirl of tornado, you experience within,
He holds you together, firmly.
With every breath of effort, you take to feel Him,
He lingers around closer, hoping to be felt by you.
But quite often we tend to look through things that are too ubiquitous?
Is that why most of us could not experience Him yet?

-found Him?

God must have stocked up gallons of love just to empty on us.
His love looks a lot like
showering us with one more chance,
being a little more patient with us,
and shedding silent tears for our fall.
How else could Je watch us through the rough days
and still trust us with another one?

-His love

Epiphanies

It's okay if you don't have a solution.
All I need is
a pair of ears to hear me out and
a pair of eyes that won't judge me after that.

-non-judgemental

If all that will ever matter
is the way you feel,
it's most important
to purify your thoughts.
Anything else is a waste of time.

–feelings

In the end,
we all will understand
it was not the rise or fall that ever mattered.
All that always mattered was the life in between
that we missed to relish
amidst the ephemeral time trials that we kept our minds busy with!

–time trails

On the days when you see yourself
heading to conquer the world,
while even picking yourself up again
seemed to be a challenge,
better understand
that's how resilience would look a lot like,
if it had a trailer!

–resilience

I choose to forgive
because hurting them back
only hurts a part of myself.
Forgiving heals.

-pain

The scars embedded in her are not marks of
imperfection.
They recite
what a warrior she has been,
that she dared to try something new,
that she fought for things that mattered to her,
and that she rose stronger every time she slipped.

–scars

Nothing tears us apart
more than experiencing deafening silence
in a space that was once filled with
laughter and endless conversations.

-old memories

What's deep down each of us is the same,
and that's what binds all of us together.

-eternity

Sometimes all the therapy
you will ever need is
a smile on your face and
a confident 'no' to the people and things
that would rob you of peace!

–therapy

I often believe
this planet would still be inhabitable
if not for those
who made you dance
when you didn't even have the strength to stand.

-better world

The greatest victory is to
surpass the expectations of the critics
so much that
the hands that turned you away once
are the same hands that
give you the loudest applause.

-bounce back

If you should mould and fold yourself
way too much just to fit in,
perhaps you don't belong in there
to begin with!

-be yourself

After being alone for long enough,
he was asked,
'What can we do for you?'
He replied,
'Smile at me when you walk past me
because for once I want to know
what it is like to be felt seen,'
with a drop of tear rolling down his cheeks.

-respect

As a part of healing,
it's all right to go through strong emotions
because you come through it
only by going through it.

-healing

As you scroll through life,
some episodes may leave you short of breath too,
but that doesn't mean the story is over.
There are still chapters waiting to gift you moments of joy
and people who will remind you of who you are.
Keep going.

-lifeline

Not everything about you is meant to be shared.
Some things are better just with you.
They are meant to go down with you
as you process them one by one.
How else could you give words to the
unspoken battles that you've fought
while the world around believed
you were doing just fine?

–secrets

Who would want to miss out on the beauty of the constellations
scattered all over the blanket of night
just by fixating on the gloomy space around it?
Likewise, I don't wish to hold on to one bad chapter in life
and let it define my destiny.
There's so much to my life than just one fall.
I am letting go of all that made me break once
so that it cannot break me once more!

–forgiveness

It's okay, mistakes happen.
Try not to be too perfect
What else could have made you discover your bravest
self but for the rough days?

It's okay to slip over and feel broken.
Try not to glue yourself back to your old-self
because somewhere between being an intact shell and
broken pieces, life happens!

It's okay to feel lost.
Try not to find your way back.
How do you think you could explore the wholesome
ways of life, if you crawled back to where you started?

It's okay to digress and goof up.
Fear not to cross paths with the unknown.
A fraction of the universe supports life only because
cosmos digressed and ran into each other, by chance.
Because it's okay!

-it's okay

www.ingramcontent.com/pod-product-compliance
Lightning Source LLC
LaVergne TN
LVHW041133150826
845673LV00007B/2303

* 9 7 9 8 8 9 2 3 3 8 3 1 8 *